Withdrawn

THE LION AND THE HARE

An
East African
Folktale

Adapted by Stephen Krensky
Illustrated by Jeni Reeves

On My Own

FOLKLORE

M Millbrook Press/Minneapolis

The illustrator thanks the Masai Mara National Reserve in Kenya and the Lincoln Park Zoo and Field Museum in Chicago, Illinois.

Text copyright © 2009 by Stephen Krensky
Illustrations copyright © 2009 by Lerner Publishing Group, Inc.

Millbrook Press
A division of Lerner Publishing Group, Inc.
241 First Avenue North
Minneapolis, MN 55401 U.S.A.

Website address: www.lernerbooks.com

Library of Congress Cataloging-in-Publication Data

Krensky, Stephen.
    The lion and the hare : an East African folktale / adapted by Stephen Krensky ; illustrated by Jeni Reeves.
        p.   cm. — (On my own folklore)
    Summary: A retelling of a traditional East African tale in which a clever hare finds a way to outwit the lion that is terrifying all the other grassland animals.
        ISBN: 978–0-8225–7546–7 (lib. bdg. : alk. paper)
    [1. Folklore—Africa, East. 2. Lions—Folklore. 3. Hares—Folklore. 4. Grassland animals—Folklore] I. Reeves, Jeni, ill. II. Title.
        PZ8.1.K8663Lio 2009
    398.2—dc22 [E]   2007013760

Manufactured in the United States of America
1 2 3 4 5 6 – DP – 14 13 12 11 10 09

*To Jolene Wood and Tony and Rosie Monkhouse of Kenya,
with whom I shared many a story and safari —J.R.*

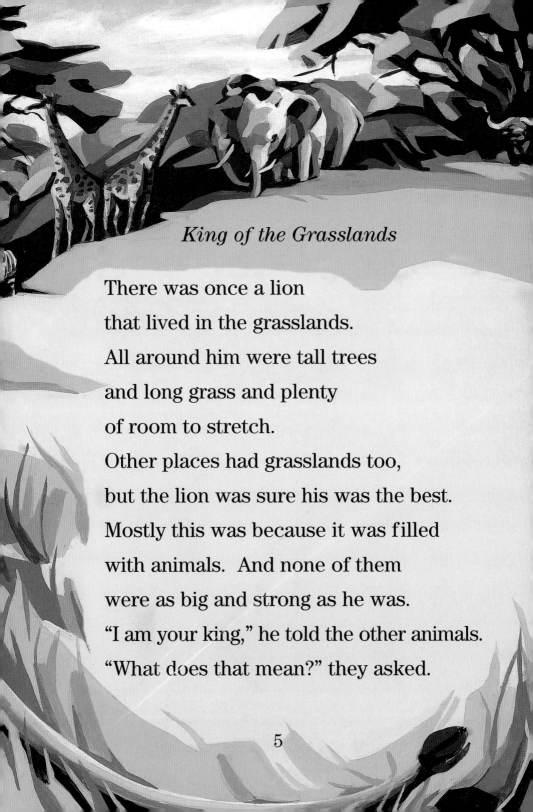

King of the Grasslands

There was once a lion
that lived in the grasslands.
All around him were tall trees
and long grass and plenty
of room to stretch.
Other places had grasslands too,
but the lion was sure his was the best.
Mostly this was because it was filled
with animals. And none of them
were as big and strong as he was.
"I am your king," he told the other animals.
"What does that mean?" they asked.

"It means I am in charge," said the lion.
"Therefore, you must do whatever I say."
The other animals did not want
to obey him, but the lion had such
sharp claws and teeth.
What else could they do?

But their problems with the lion
were only just beginning.
He made things even worse
because every day he hunted down
some animals—and ate them.
Sometimes he ate one.
Sometimes he ate two.
And sometimes, he was so hungry,
he just kept eating and eating.

Naturally, the remaining animals
were very upset.
"I can hardly sleep," said the hedgehog.
"I'm always looking over my
shoulder," said the giraffe.
"I don't even have any shoulders,"
said the snake.
"Never mind all that," said the chimpanzee.
"We have to do something."
The others nodded.
If the lion went on this way, pretty soon
there would be no other animals left.
But what could they do?
The animals were not sure.
So they held a meeting
to discuss their choices.

"It wouldn't be so bad if we just had
to bow when he went by,"
said the wild pig.
"Or call him 'Your Majesty,'"
said the antelope.
"It's his appetite we have to
worry about," said the zebra.

The animals talked things over
long into the night.
And by morning,
they were all very sleepy.
But they knew what they had to do.

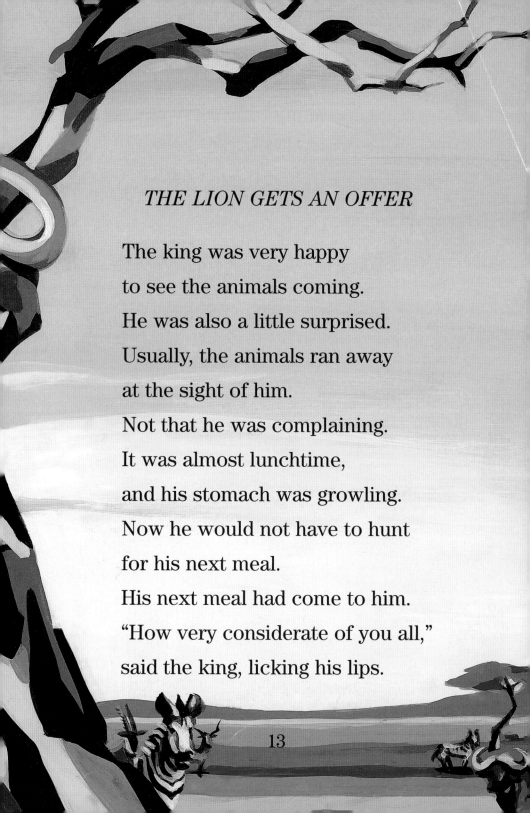

THE LION GETS AN OFFER

The king was very happy
to see the animals coming.
He was also a little surprised.
Usually, the animals ran away
at the sight of him.
Not that he was complaining.
It was almost lunchtime,
and his stomach was growling.
Now he would not have to hunt
for his next meal.
His next meal had come to him.
"How very considerate of you all,"
said the king, licking his lips.

"Hold on," said the chimpanzee,
who was leading the group.
"Don't pounce quite yet.
Listen to what we have to say.
You are the king of the grasslands.
Correct?"
"Of course," said the lion.

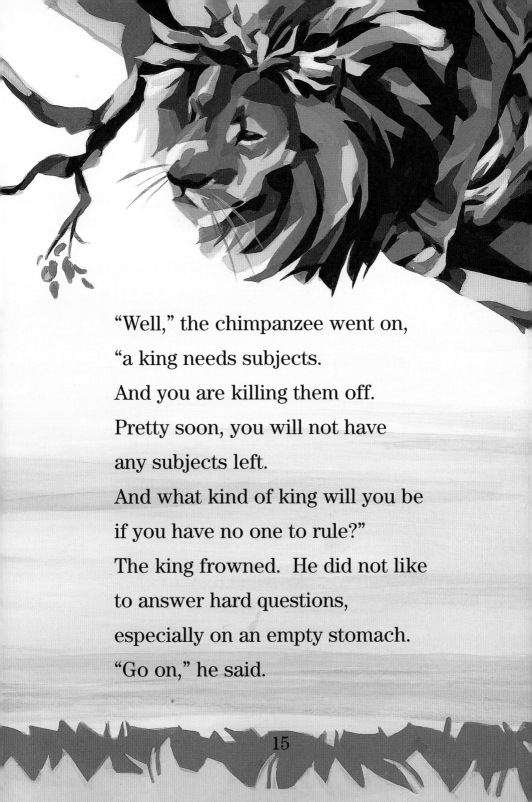

"Well," the chimpanzee went on,
"a king needs subjects.
And you are killing them off.
Pretty soon, you will not have
any subjects left.
And what kind of king will you be
if you have no one to rule?"
The king frowned. He did not like
to answer hard questions,
especially on an empty stomach.
"Go on," he said.

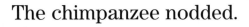

The chimpanzee nodded.

"We have an idea.

First, you must agree to stop

hunting us."

The king laughed.

"Why would I do that?"

"Because it's not dignified,"

said the chimpanzee.

"A king should not have to hunt

for his dinner.

He should not have to run and hide

in the bushes.

A king should lie in a patch of sun

all day.

And then, when he is hungry,

his dinner should arrive

at just the right time."

The king smiled.

He was very fond of patches of sun.

And sometimes, he caught thorns in his paws while waiting in the bushes.

Clearly, the chimpanzee was making good sense.

But he still had a question.

"If I do not hunt for my dinner,
how will I get it?"
"It will come to you,"
said the chimpanzee.
All the other animals nodded.
"Every day, we will send you
one animal to eat."

The king smiled.

He was very lazy at heart.

"I will agree to your terms," he said,

"but I have one thing to add.

If my dinner does not come one day,

then I will hunt you all down

and finish you off."

The other animals sighed.
They were not happy, but they were
making the best of a bad situation.
"We understand," they said.

THE DINNER THAT SAID NO

From then on, one animal was sent

to the lion each day.

The grasslands were a sad place,

but the lion paid no attention.

He was fat and happy,

and nothing else mattered to him.

Then one morning,

a hare got some news.

It was very bad news.

His turn had come to be the lion's dinner.

"This is a great honor,"

the other animals told him.

"I am not looking for honor," the hare said.

"I don't want to be the lion's dinner.

I just want my own dinner."

"It does not matter what you want,"
said the other animals.
"If we do not keep our promise,
the lion will eat us all."
"It matters to me,"
the hare said to himself.
He needed a plan,
and he needed it fast.

A little later, the hare slowly
hopped toward the lion's den.
He felt nervous.
Watching the lion pace back and forth
didn't make him feel any better.
"What do you want?" the king snarled.
"I am waiting for my dinner."

"Yes, well, that's why I'm here,"
the hare explained.
"I am your dinner."
"You? YOU!"
The king was furious.
"I am hungry! Very hungry!
Do you understand that?"

The hare was not going to argue.

"And being hungry, I was expecting

more than one little hare."

The hare nodded quickly.

"I am sure you were.

And so was I.

Actually, there were six of us at first."

"Six hares?"

The lion stopped to think.

"That would not be so bad."

He looked around.

"So where are the others?"

The hare sighed.

"They wanted to be here.

Really.

But then *he* appeared.

The other lion, I mean."

"Another lion?"

The king looked confused.

"Exactly," said the hare.

"And he ate the other five hares.

He would have eaten me too,

but he left me alive to give you a message."

The king roared.

"A message? What did he say?"

"He said you were an impostor.
He said you were not a real king
of the beasts.
He said you were not even the king
of your own shadow."

"I see."

The hare took a deep breath.

"He said you were just a big bully
and a lazy ball of fur."

"I see."

"He said—"

"Never mind," the king snapped.

"I get the message."

He raked his claws on the ground.

"Makes threats, does he?

Throws insults, does he?

I'm going to give this lion

a message of my own.

Can you lead me to him?"

The hare nodded.

THE LION MEETS HIS MATCH

The lion and the hare raced
through the grasslands.
"How much farther?"
the king demanded.
"We're almost there," said the hare.
Soon they reached the edge of a well.
"Why have we stopped?" the king asked.
"The lion's in there," the hare whispered.
He pointed to the well.
"What's he doing down there?"
asked the king.
"Waiting," the hare explained.
"I think he plans to jump out
at you after you pass by."

"We'll see about that," said the king.

Cautiously, he walked to the well

and looked over the edge.

There in the water

he saw another lion.

And this lion was looking at him

just as he was looking at it.

The second lion looked pretty fierce,

the king had to admit.

But looks were not everything.

He bared his sharp teeth.

The other lion did the same.

He let out a roar.

And a roar echoed back at him.

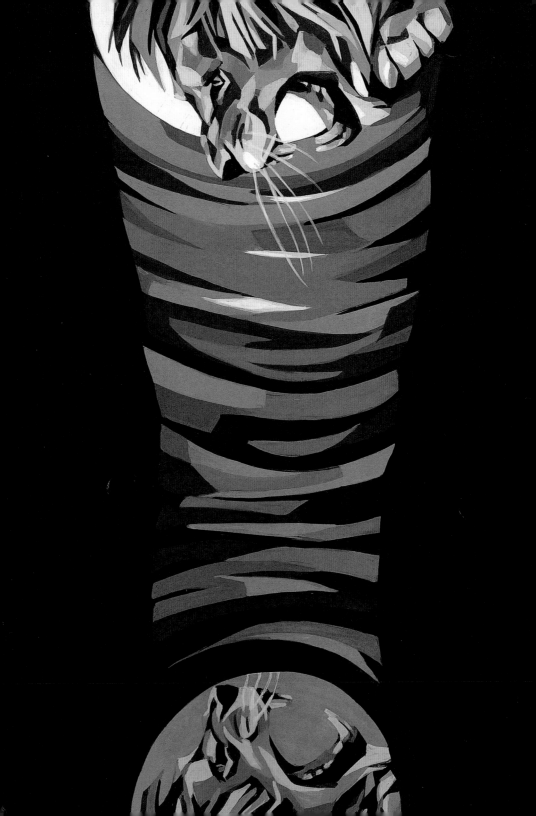

The king was not ready
to back down.
This was his kingdom,
and he would not give it up.

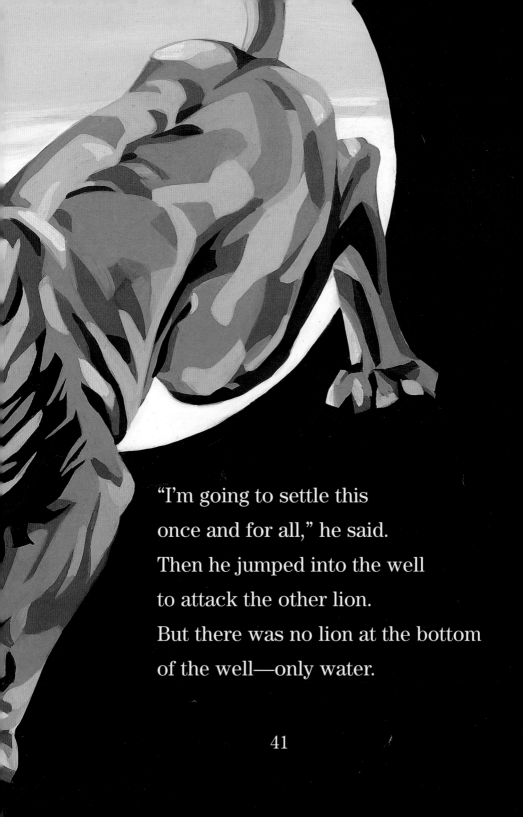

"I'm going to settle this
once and for all," he said.
Then he jumped into the well
to attack the other lion.
But there was no lion at the bottom
of the well—only water.

"I've been tricked!" he shouted.

"You are in big trouble now, hare."

"Luckily, I'm not the only one,"
the hare replied.

This made the king even madder.

He splashed about, muttering about
what he was going to do to the hare
once he got his paws on him.

But he never got the chance.

For in the next moment,
the king hit his head
on the side of the well and drowned.

The little hare wrinkled his nose.
Then he went back to the other animals
to tell them the news.
When they heard the hare's tale,
they were amazed.

They wanted to make the hare
the king of beasts.
But he refused.
"All I want is my dinner," he said,
and he hopped off to find it.

Afterword

You just read a folktale. A folktale is a story told by common people. People all around the world have told folktales for thousands of years. Folktales often explain something about the world around us or teach a lesson. Can you think of a lesson that this story teaches?

People in several different parts of the world have told this tale of a mean lion and a clever hare. In India, the story features a rabbit and a lion. Lions were once common in India. They are a little smaller than the lions that live in Africa.

In the United States, people tell a similar tale about characters named Brer Rabbit and Boss Lion. One version of the story takes place in Louisiana. Brer Rabbit is a character in many African American folktales. He is a trickster—a character who plays tricks to get what he wants. By tricking the lion, he makes life safer for all the other animals.

In this book, the story is set in East Africa. The hare has friends who are animals that live on the grasslands. Can you imagine what this story might be like if it took place in a different part of the world?

Glossary

bared: showed

bow: to bend the head or body down to show respect

dignified: formal and proper

grasslands: also called the savanna. This environment has long grasses and scattered trees and shrubs.

hedgehog: a small animal that has hair and spines sticking out of its skin

pounce: to jump on something and grab onto it

well: a deep hole in the ground with water at the bottom

Further Reading and Websites

Books

Anderson, Jill. *Lions.* Minnetonka, MN: NorthWord, 2006.
This short book features colorful photos of lions and basic facts.

Dunphy, Madeline. *Here Is the African Savanna.* New York: Hyperion
    Books for Children, 1999.
Learn more about the many animals that live on the African grasslands.

Kessler, Brad. *Brer Rabbit and Boss Lion.* Rowayton, CT: Rabbit Ears
    Books, 2005. Distributed by ABDO Pub.
This story of a mean lion and a clever rabbit is set in the United States.

Knutson, Barbara. *Sungura and Leopard: A Swahili Trickster Tale.*
    Minneapolis: First Avenue Editions, 2007.
Here is an East African tale of a trickster rabbit. In this tale, he must out-
    smart a hungry leopard.

Websites

African Savanna—National Zoo
http://nationalzoo.si.edu/Animals/AfricanSavanna/
This area of the National Zoo's website has information on many of the
    animals that live on the African savanna. You can also find out which
    African animals are at the zoo.

Hare Coloring Page
http://www.first-school.ws/t/cphare.htm
You can print out this outline of a hare and color it yourself.